ELEMENTARY

SCAT

Grades 2-3

2023

Larchmont Academics

LarchmontAcademics.com

To request permissions or inquire about buying this title in bulk, contact the publisher.

ISBN: 9798360062615

Second paperback edition.

The School and College Ability Test (SCAT) is owned and operated by The Johns Hopkins Center for Talented Youth, which was not involved in the production of, and does not endorse, sponsor, or certify this product.

Neither the author or publisher claim any responsibility for the accuracy and appropriateness of the content in this book, nor do they claim any responsibility over the outcome of students who use these materials.

Published in the USA

Larchmont Academics
Los Angeles, CA

LarchmontAcademics.com

Table of Contents

Preparing for the Test

What to Expect on the SCAT

The SCAT has two sections: Verbal and Quantitative. This book will prepare you for both sections.

Each section is 22 minutes long and contains 55 questions.

Verbal Section
Tests your understanding of meaning through word analogies. The goal is to determine the relationship between the word pair. You then must find another word pair with a similar relationship.

Example:

1. good : great
     a. tremendous : amazing
     b. bad : terrible
     c. pretty : ugly
     d. nice : proud

Answer: B
Good is a lower degree of *great*. *Bad* is a lower degree of *terrible*.

Quantitative Section
Tests your mathematical reasoning skills. The goal is to determine which value is greater or if both values are equal. Many of the questions do not require computation. Instead, the goal is to determine the answer through reasoning

Example:

Column A	Column B
$5 \times 4 \times 3 \times 0$	$1 \times 4 \times 2$

Answer: Column B is greater.
Column A is being multiplied by 0. Any number being multiplied by 0 will be 0. Column B will be larger than 0.

Strategies for the Verbal Section

Goal

Your goal is to determine the relationship between the word pair and then find a pair with a similar relationship.

1. pear : fruit
   a. cactus : fern
   b. dog : animal
   c. drink : food
   d. house : apartment

Connecting the Words

Create a simple sentence that shows the connection between the two words.

Example:

pear : fruit → A pear **is a type of** fruit.

Avoid simply saying "A pear is a fruit" because it is not specific enough.

Check the Answer Choices

Check the answer choices using your sentence.

    X Cactus is a type of fern

    ✓ dog is a type of animal

    X drink is a type of food

    X house is a type of apartment

Answer : B – A dog is a type of animal.

Common Relationships

Look for these common relationships.

_____ is the same as _____

_____ is the opposite of _____

_____ is a type of _____

_____ is a higher/lesser degree of _____

_____ is the function of _____

_____ is a tool for _____

_____ is a person who _____

Strategies for the Quantitative Section

Goal

Your goal is to compare the value of Column A with the value of Column B.

1.

Column A	Column B
$12 + 14 + 44 + 4$	$13 + 15 + 24 + 8$

You will choose from three answer choices:
   A) Column A is greater
   B) Column B is greater
   C) Columns A and B are equal

Compare, don't <u>always</u> solve!

Often, you will not need to solve both column A and B to find the answer, instead, compare both sides.

Column A	Column B
$12 + 14 + 44 + 4$ 44 is **twenty** higher than 24	$13 + 15 + 24 + 8$ 13 is **one** higher than 12 15 is **one** higher than 14 8 is **four** higher than 4

Column A is greater because the twenty in Column A is much higher than the differences in Column B

Be ready for common tricky question types!

Here are some common rules to know and be ready for!

Powers and Multiplication

$1^{48} = 1$ → 1 to the power of anything is 1

$0^{34} = 0$ → 0 to the power of anything is 0

$5 \times 12 \times 3 \times 0 \times 23 = 0$ → Anything × 0 = 0

$40 \times 5 = 4 \times 50$ → Break up the multiplication to see it is equal
$$4 \times 10 \times 5 = 4 \times 5 \times 10$$

Fractions and Decimals

$\frac{4}{5} > \frac{3}{5}$ → if the denominators are the same, the one with the larger numerator is the larger fraction

$\frac{4}{7} > \frac{4}{9}$ → if the numerators are the same, the one with the smaller denominator is larger fraction

$\frac{4}{11} < \frac{6}{7}$ → if neither are the same, decide if the fractions are larger than half, half, or less than half

4×0.8 → a whole number × a decimal will make that whole number smaller

Unit Comparisons

1000 millimeters = 1 meter
100 centimeters = 1 meter
1000 meters = 1 kilometer

12 inches = 1 foot
1 yard = 3 feet

Look at the answer explanations to learn other tips and strategies!

Timing Strategies

Keep Track of Your Timing

You only have 24 seconds per question. Some questions will take much less time than this and others will take much more. Instead of watching the clock at every question, check the clock after 10 questions. If you have 18 minutes to go or more, you are at a good pace. If not, work on moving at a faster pace. The best thing to do to work on your timing is to practice.

Every 4 minutes, you should be 10 questions further along.

Know when to guess and move on!

Unlike in school, you do not need to show work and be absolutely sure of your answer. Instead, the goal is to reason and make an assessment based on the information given. So, if you don't know something, take your best guess based on what you do know.

Practice Test #1

Verbal Test #1

55 Questions – 22 Minutes

1. hands : clap
   A) phone : on
   B) eyelids : blink
   C) feet : big
   D) shirt : red

2. fish : swim
   A) bird : fly
   B) rhinoceros : snort
   C) pig : oink
   D) cow : moo

3. hammer : nails
   A) build : destroy
   B) plastic : wood
   C) stone: straw
   D) needle : thread

4. pen : ink
   A) write : paper
   B) read : book
   C) pencil : lead
   D) sew : fabric

5. admiration : awe
   A) peace : calm
   B) sadness : joy
   C) anger : thankfulness
   D) evil : good

6. control : variable

    A) steps : method

    B) purpose : goal

    C) similarity : difference

    D) optional : choice

7. school : desk

    A) chair : cushion

    B) church : pew

    C) screw : screwdriver

    D) nails : polish

8. teeth : toothbrush

    A) hair : long

    B) dirty : laundry

    C) dishes : dishwasher

    D) shoe : sock

9. pillow : blanket

    A) sugar : salt

    B) love : hate

    C) hat : scarf

    D) water : tea

10. dog : puppy

    A) frog : pony

    B) pig : piglet

    C) cat : lion

    D) jackal : dingo

11. hypothesis : prediction

    A) theory : practice

    B) introduction : content

    C) summary : synopsis

    D) method : goal

12. painter : painting

    A) teacher : teaches

    B) sailor : sails

    C) carpenter : carves

    D) sculptor : sculpture

13. whale : baleen

    A) snake : fangs

    B) ocean : water

    C) monkey : gorilla

    D) window : panes

14. pear : fruit

    A) eat : healthy

    B) soup : smoothie

    C) bread : pasta

    D) celery : vegetable

15. outside : inside

    A) tall : big

    B) wet : damp

    C) open : closed

    D) dry : arid

16. sock : foot

    A) jacket : coat

    B) shirt : pants

    C) glove : hand

    D) boots : shoes

17. angles : degrees

    A) lines : inches

    B) many : few

    C) vertices : points

    D) edges : height

18. caldron : pot

    A) fire : flame

    B) water : soda

    C) hammer : ax

    D) spoon : fork

19. light fixture : chandelier

    A) candle : flashlight

    B) fish : trout

    C) sunrise : sunset

    D) winter : spring

20. window : view

    A) door : exit

    B) bedroom : kitchen

    C) ceiling : floor

    D) walls : vents

21. right : left

    A) wrong : incorrect

    B) enter : come

    C) wet : damp

    D) east : west

22. horse : bridle

    A) pig : snout

    B) donkey : ears

    C) mouse : whiskers

    D) dog : collar

23. ears : two

    A) toes : ten

    B) feet : small

    C) eyes : dark

    D) ankle : weak

24. violin : bow

    A) trumpet : cold

    B) drum : drumstick

    C) flute : metal

    D) xylophone : bell

25. add : subtract

    A) fill : full

    B) gather : disperse

    C) answer : choose

    D) math : science

26. warning : caution

    A) news : announcements

    B) rules : broken

    C) plans : changed

    D) promises : kept

27. verb : run

    A) preposition : and

    B) true : false

    C) noun : chair

    D) conjunction : with

28. lion : roar

    A) hope : deferred

    B) joy : found

    C) thunder : silent

    D) bell : ring

29. arm : elbow

    A) feet : hurt

    B) head : round

    C) fingers : fast

    D) leg : knee

30. giggle : cackle

    A) hum : sing

    B) snicker : cry

    C) chortle : snark

    D) drink : eat

31. representative : ambassador

    A) leader : follower

    B) inventor : tradesman

    C) rebel : dissenter

    D) servant : pilgrim

32. mammal : whale

    A) reptile : lizard

    B) willow : tree

    C) holly : bush

    D) pepper : spice

33. wonderful : fabulous

    A) climb : fall

    B) unearth : bury

    C) stupendous : marvelous

    D) negative : positive

34. pacify : calm

    A) anger : infuriate

    B) hurt : heal

    C) mend : tear

    D) help : hinder

35. tax : tariff

    A) war : peace

    B) rights : liberties

    C) react : instigate

    D) negotiate : threaten

36. odd : even

   A) consonant : vowel

   B) finicky : picky

   C) whimsical : impulsive

   D) complete : whole

37. milk : yogurt

   A) crackers : crunchy

   B) fruit : sweet

   C) cereal : soggy

   D) egg : omelet

38. school : principal

   A) team : player

   B) group : member

   C) church : congregants

   D) company : boss

39. stove : oven

   A) refrigerator : freezer

   B) garage : bathroom

   C) basement : gym

   D) pool : closet

40. exercise : active

   A) feed : water

   B) math : spelling

   C) rest : still

   D) work : hard

41. root : stem

   A) grass : weeds

   B) growing : rotten

   C) plant : harvest

   D) trunk : branches

42. transformation : metamorphosis

   A) disarray : organized

   B) burn : scald

   C) final : first

   D) flower : seed

43. longitude : latitude

   A) equator : hot

   B) poles : cold

   C) vertical : horizontal

   D) over : above

44. librarian : books

   A) driver : rain

   B) plumber : pipes

   C) mechanic : mop

   D) barber : nails

45. abandon : desert

   A) unite : join

   B) come : leave

   C) consume : waste

   D) exist : extinct

46. caterpillars : butterflies

   A) bees : flies

   B) worms : snakes

   C) spiders : scorpions

   D) tadpoles : frogs

47. cucumbers : pickles

   A) beans : green

   B) fruit : jam

   C) corn : cob

   D) meat : spicy

48. confidence : arrogance

   A) worry : joy

   B) hate : love

   C) trust : assurance

   D) fear : playfulness

49. appetites : desires

   A) reality : dreams

   B) function : form

   C) values : beliefs

   D) ancient : fresh

50. river : stream

   A) ocean : sea

   B) inlet : mountain

   C) hill : well

   D) sink : swim

51. break : brake

    A) grow : blossom

    B) blank : full

    C) bark : below

    D) knew : new

52. secondary : green

    A) cool : warm

    B) complement : clash

    C) suggest : demand

    D) primary : red

53. treble : high

    A) tenor : alto

    B) harmony : melody

    C) bass : low

    D) sing : chant

54. sedimentary : igneous

    A) geology : rocks

    B) pineapple : orange

    C) botany : plants

    D) anatomy : body

55. knob : handle

    A) chair : seat

    B) rope : lever

    C) comet : planet

    D) finish : start

Verbal Test #1 – Answers

1. B	20. A	39. A
2. A	21. D	40. C
3. D	22. D	41. D
4. C	23. A	42. B
5. A	24. B	43. C
6. C	25. B	44. B
7. B	26. A	45. A
8. C	27. C	46. D
9. C	28. D	47. B
10. B	29. D	48. C
11. C	30. A	49. C
12. D	31. C	50. A
13. A	32. A	51. D
14. D	33. C	52. D
15. C	34. A	53. C
16. C	35. B	54. B
17. A	36. A	55. A
18. A	37. D	
19. B	38. D	

Verbal Test #1 – Explanations

1. Answer: B
   Hands clap **when put together.**
   Eyelids blink **when put together.**

2. Answer: A
   Fish **travel by** swimming.
   Birds **travel by** flying.

3. Answer: D
   Hammer and nails **are tools that must be used together.**
   Needle and thread **are tools that must be used together.**

4. Answer: C
   A pen **uses** ink **to write.**
   A pencil **uses** lead **to write.**

5. Answer: A
   Admiration **is the same as** awe.
   Peace **is the same as** calm.

6. Answer: C
   Control **is the opposite of** variable.
   Similarity **is the opposite of** difference.

7. Answer: B
   At school **one sits in a** desk.
   At a church **one sits in a** pew.

8. Answer: C
   Teeth **are cleaned using a** toothbrush.
   Dishes **are cleaned using a** dishwasher.

9. Answer: C
   A pillow **pairs with a** blanket.
   A hat **pairs with a** scarf.

10. Answer: B
    A dog **gives birth to** puppies.
    A pig **gives birth to** piglets.

11. Answer: C

A hypothesis **is the same as a** prediction.
A summary **is the same as a** synopsis.

12. Answer: D

A painter **produces a** painting.
A sculptor **produces a** sculpture.

13. Answer: A

A whale **has specialized teeth called** baleen.
A snake **has specialized teeth called** fangs.

14. Answer: D

A pear **is a type of** fruit.
Celery **is a type of** vegetable.

15. Answer: C

Outside **is the opposite of** inside.
Open **is the opposite of** closed.

16. Answer: C

A sock **goes on one's** foot.
A glove **goes on one's** hand.

17. Answer: A

Angles **can be measured with** degrees.
Lines **can be measured with** inches.

18. Answer: A

Kettle **is a large** pot.
Fire **is a large** flame.

19. Answer: B

A chandelier **is a type of** light fixture.
A trout **is a type of** fish.

20. Answer: A

A window **provides a** view.
A door **provides an** exit.

21. Answer: D
    Right **is the opposite of** left.
    East **is the opposite of** west.

22. Answer: D
    A horse **wears a** bridle.
    A dog **wears a** collar.

23. Answer: A
    Humans usually have 2 ears.
    Humans usually have 10 toes.

24. Answer: B
    A violin **is played with a** bow.
    A drum **is played with a** drumstick.

25. Answer: B
    Add **is the opposite of** subtract.
    Gather **is the opposite of** disperse

26. Answer: A
    Warning **is similar to** caution.
    News **is similar to** announcements.

27. Answer: C
    Run **is a** verb.
    Chair **is a** noun.

28. Answer: D
    Lions **make a noise called a** roar.
    Bells **make a noise called a** ring.

29. Answer: D
    Arms **bend at the** elbow.
    Legs **bend at the** knee.

30. Answer: A
    To giggle **is a lower degree than** to cackle.
    To hum **is a lower degree than** to sing.

31. Answer: C
    Representative **is the same as** an ambassador.
    Rebel **is the same as** dissenter.

32. Answer: A

    One type of mammal is a whale.

    One type of reptile is a lizard.

33. Answer: C

    Wonderful **is the same as** fabulous.

    Stupendous **is the same as** with marvelous.

34. Answer: A

    To pacify **means to** calm.

    To anger **means to** infuriate.

35. Answer: B

    Tax **is the same as** tariff.

    Rights **are the same as** liberties.

36. Answer: A

    Odd **is the opposite of** even.

    Consonants **are the opposite of** vowels.

37. Answer: D

    Milk **is needed to make** yogurt.

    Eggs **are needed to make** omelets.

38. Answer: D

    At a school the principal **is in charge.**

    At a company, the boss **is in charge**.

39. Answer: A

    A stove **goes with an** oven.

    A refrigerator **goes with a** freezer.

40. Answer: C

    Exercise **involves being** active.

    Rest **involves being** still.

41. Answer: D

    Plant roots **lead to** stems.

    Tree trunks **lead to** branches.

42. Answer: B

Metamorphosis **is a type of** transformation.
A scald **is a type of** burn.

43. Answer: C

Longitude and latitude **lines go together to create a grid.**
Vertical and horizontal **lines go together to create a grid.**

44. Answer: B

A librarian **works with** books.
A plumber **works with** pipes.

45. Answer: A

Abandon **means to** desert.
Unite **means to** join.

46. Answer: D

Caterpillars **turn into** butterflies.
Tadpoles **turn into** frogs.

47. Answers: B

Cucumbers **can become** pickles.
Fruit **can become** jam.

48. Answers: C

Confidence **can lead to** arrogance.
Trust **can lead to** assurance.

49. Answers: C

Appetites and desires **are synonyms.**
Values and beliefs **are synonyms.**

50. Answers: A

Rivers **are bigger bodies of water than** streams.
Oceans **are bigger bodies of water than** seas.

51. Answers: D

Break and brake **are homophones.**
Knew and new **are homophones.**

52. Answers: D

Green **is a** secondary **color.**
Red **is a** primary **color.**

53. Answers: C

Treble clef **mostly includes** high notes.
Bass clef **mostly includes** low notes.

54. Answers: B

Sedimentary and igneous **are both types of rocks.**
Pineapple and orange **are both types of fruits.**

55. Answers: A

A knob **is another word for** handle.
A chair **is another word for** seat.

Quantitative Reasoning Test #1

55 Questions – 22 Minutes

1.

Column A	Column B
22 × 12	13 × 24

A) Column A is greater.

B) Column B is greater.

C) Columns A and B are equal.

2.

Column A	Column B
13 + 24 + 56 + 3	16 + 28 + 26 + 2

A) Column A is greater.

B) Column B is greater.

C) Columns A and B are equal.

3.

Column A	Column B
2 feet 3 inches	27 inches

A) Column A is greater.

B) Column B is greater.

C) Columns A and B are equal.

4.

Column A	Column B
$3^2 + 1^8$	$3^2 + 1^{12}$

A) Column A is greater.

B) Column B is greater.

C) Columns A and B are equal.

5.

Column A	Column B
$\dfrac{5}{8}$	$\dfrac{5}{7}$

A) Column A is greater.

B) Column B is greater.

C) Columns A and B are equal.

6.

Column A	Column B
$\dfrac{1}{8} + \dfrac{5}{8}$	$\dfrac{2}{16} + \dfrac{9}{16}$

A) Column A is greater.

B) Column B is greater.

C) Columns A and B are equal.

7.

Column A	Column B
54	Total amount Ava spent in dollars if she spent $20.50 on a shirt, $30.50 on a dress, and $4 on a snack

A) Column A is greater.

B) Column B is greater.

C) Columns A and B are equal.

8.

Column A	Column B
The fraction of the pizza left if the family ate 5/6 of the pizza	The fraction of cake left if the family ate 4/7 of the cake

A) Column A is greater.

B) Column B is greater.

C) Columns A and B are equal.

9.

Column A	Column B
Round to the nearest hundred: 406.	1600 ÷ 4

A) Column A is greater.

B) Column B is greater.

C) Columns A and B are equal.

10.

Column A	Column B
54×5	$54 + 54 + 54 + 54$

A) Column A is greater.

B) Column B is greater.

C) Columns A and B are equal.

11.

Column A	Column B
The value of x	The value of y
$4x = 16$	$12 - y = 8$

A) Column A is greater.

B) Column B is greater.

C) Columns A and B are equal.

12.

Column A	Column B
$3 + 2 \times 5$	$(3 + 2) \times 5$

A) Column A is greater.

B) Column B is greater.

C) Columns A and B are equal.

13.

Column A	Column B
12×8	24×4

A) Column A is greater.

B) Column B is greater.

C) Columns A and B are equal.

14.

Column A	Column B
The fraction of cake remaining if Sam gave half to Kara and one forth to Maya	$\dfrac{1}{5} + \dfrac{3}{5}$

A) Column A is greater.

B) Column B is greater.

C) Columns A and B are equal.

15.

Column A	Column B
The next whole number after 112	The next odd number after 111

A) Column A is greater.

B) Column B is greater.

C) Columns A and B are equal.

16.

Column A	Column B
LCM of (5, 7)	GCF of (30, 10)

A) Column A is greater.

B) Column B is greater.

C) Columns A and B are equal.

17.

Column A	Column B
The distance around the shape if each side is 4 inches	The distance around the shape if each side is 4 inches

A) Column A is greater.

B) Column B is greater.

C) Columns A and B are equal.

18.

Column A	Column B
$1600 - 540$	$1599 - 640$

A) Column A is greater.

B) Column B is greater.

C) Columns A and B are equal.

19.

Column A	Column B
$5 \times 8 \times 4 \times 0 \times 2$	3×2

A) Column A is greater.

B) Column B is greater.

C) Columns A and B are equal.

20.

Column A	Column B
The value of x $6 + x = 22$	The value of y $y \div 2 = 9$

A) Column A is greater.

B) Column B is greater.

C) Columns A and B are equal.

21.

Column A	Column B
The next prime number after 5	$\sqrt{36}$

A) Column A is greater.

B) Column B is greater.

C) Columns A and B are equal.

22.

Column A	Column B
1.2×6	2.8×3

A) Column A is greater.

B) Column B is greater.

C) Columns A and B are equal.

23.

Column A	Column B
0.8×10	80×0.1

A) Column A is greater.

B) Column B is greater.

C) Columns A and B are equal.

24.

Column A	Column B
$1^{45} + 0^{32}$	$2^3 + 0^3$

A) Column A is greater.

B) Column B is greater.

C) Columns A and B are equal.

25.

Column A	Column B
The value of x $x - 4 = 14$	The value of y $6 \times y = 18$

A) Column A is greater.

B) Column B is greater.

C) Columns A and B are equal.

26.

Column A	Column B
$4.526 + 3.1$	$5.2 + 2.1$

A) Column A is greater.

B) Column B is greater.

C) Columns A and B are equal.

27.

Column A	Column B
$345 + 431$	$305 + 481$

A) Column A is greater.

B) Column B is greater.

C) Columns A and B are equal.

28.

Column A	Column B
The number of thousands in 4304	The number of hundreds in 2921

A) Column A is greater.

B) Column B is greater.

C) Columns A and B are equal.

29.

Column A	Column B
$128 + 24$	$127 + 26$

A) Column A is greater.

B) Column B is greater.

C) Columns A and B are equal.

30.

Column A	Column B
$308 - 45 - 50$	200

A) Column A is greater.

B) Column B is greater.

C) Columns A and B are equal.

31.

Column A	Column B
$436 - 48$	$336 + 34$

A) Column A is greater.

B) Column B is greater.

C) Columns A and B are equal.

32.

Column A	Column B
The next number in the series:	6×6
4, 12, 20, 28, ___	

A) Column A is greater.

B) Column B is greater.

C) Columns A and B are equal.

33.

Column A	Column B
1000 meters	1 kilometer

A) Column A is greater.

B) Column B is greater.

C) Columns A and B are equal.

34.

Column A	Column B
Number of angles in the shape below:	Number of angles in the shape below:

A) Column A is greater.

B) Column B is greater.

C) Columns A and B are equal.

35.

Column A	Column B
$\dfrac{7}{6}$	$\dfrac{1}{2} + \dfrac{1}{2} + \dfrac{1}{6} - \dfrac{1}{3}$

A) Column A is greater.

B) Column B is greater.

C) Columns A and B are equal.

36.

Column A	Column B
2 ½ hours	130 minutes

A) Column A is greater.

B) Column B is greater.

C) Columns A and B are equal.

37.

Column A	Column B
54	8 tens and 2 ones

A) Column A is greater.

B) Column B is greater.

C) Columns A and B are equal.

38.

Column A	Column B
The next odd number after 63	The next even number after 63

A) Column A is greater.

B) Column B is greater.

C) Columns A and B are equal.

39.

Column A	Column B
The missing number in the series 1, 3, 9, ___, 81	The missing number in the series 22, 28, ___, 40

A) Column A is greater.

B) Column B is greater.

C) Columns A and B are equal.

40.

Column A	Column B
0.4	$\dfrac{4}{5}$

A) Column A is greater.

B) Column B is greater.

C) Columns A and B are equal.

41.

Column A	Column B
20	$\dfrac{1}{3}$ of 60

A) Column A is greater.

B) Column B is greater.

C) Columns A and B are equal.

42.

Column A	Column B
The value of h $h \times 4 = 12$	$\dfrac{3}{2}$

A) Column A is greater.

B) Column B is greater.

C) Columns A and B are equal.

43.

Column A	Column B
The area of a rectangle with a length of 2 and a width of 5	The area of a rectangle with a length of 1 and a width of 6

A) Column A is greater.

B) Column B is greater.

C) Columns A and B are equal.

44. A five pack of chocolate bars costs $2.50.

Column A	Column B
The price of one chocolate bar	$0.99

A) Column A is greater.

B) Column B is greater.

C) Columns A and B are equal.

45.

Column A	Column B
40×5	50×4

A) Column A is greater.

B) Column B is greater.

C) Columns A and B are equal.

46.

Column A	Column B
$\dfrac{4}{5} + \dfrac{1}{5} + \dfrac{3}{5}$	2

A) Column A is greater.

B) Column B is greater.

C) Columns A and B are equal.

47.

Column A	Column B
0.4×0.2	0.4

A) Column A is greater.

B) Column B is greater.

C) Columns A and B are equal.

48. Sarah caught fewer fish than Anya. Sarah caught more fish than Jaden.

Column A	Column B
The amount of fish Jaden caught	The amount of fish Anya caught

A) Column A is greater.

B) Column B is greater.

C) Columns A and B are equal.

49.

Column A	Column B
The value of 3 dimes and one nickel	The value of five nickels, one dime, and one penny

A) Column A is greater.

B) Column B is greater.

C) Columns A and B are equal.

50.

Column A	Column B
$4 \times 4 \times 4$	4^4

A) Column A is greater.

B) Column B is greater.

C) Columns A and B are equal.

51.

Column A	Column B
10% *of* 200	5% *of* 120

A) Column A is greater.

B) Column B is greater.

C) Columns A and B are equal.

52. Data set:
    4, 5, 5, 5, 8, 8, 9, 10, 10

Column A	Column B
The mode	The median

A) Column A is greater.

B) Column B is greater.

C) Columns A and B are equal.

53.

Column A	Column B
The number in the tenths place 2.432	The number in the hundredths place 2.432

A) Column A is greater.

B) Column B is greater.

C) Columns A and B are equal.

54.

Column A	Column B
$\sqrt{49}$	$-16 \div 2$

A) Column A is greater.

B) Column B is greater.

C) Columns A and B are equal.

55.

Column A	Column B
The remainder of $44 \div 10$	2^3

A) Column A is greater.

B) Column B is greater.

C) Columns A and B are equal.

Quantitative Test #1 – Answers

1. B	20. B	39. B
2. A	21. A	40. B
3. C	22. B	41. C
4. C	23. C	42. A
5. B	24. B	43. A
6. A	25. A	44. B
7. B	26. A	45. C
8. B	27. B	46. B
9. C	28. B	47. B
10. A	29. B	48. B
11. C	30. A	49. B
12. A	31. A	50. B
13. C	32. C	51. A
14. B	33. C	52. B
15. C	34. B	53. A
16. A	35. A	54. A
17. A	36. A	55. B
18. A	37. B	
19. B	38. A	

Quantitative Test #1 - Explanations

1. **B**

Column A	Column B
22×12	13×24
	13 is larger than 12.
	24 is larger than 22.

2. **A**

Column A	Column B
$13 + 24 + 56 + 3$	$16 + 28 + 26 + 2$
96 is much larger than all numbers in column B.	

3. **C**

Column A	Column B
2 feet 3 inches	27 inches
2 feet = 24 inches	
24 + 3 = 27 inches	

4. **C**

Column A	Column B
$3^2 + 1^8$	$3^2 + 1^{12}$
1 to the power of anything is 1.	
$3^2 + 1$	$3^2 + 1$

5. **B**

Column A	Column B
$\dfrac{5}{8}$	$\dfrac{5}{7}$

Given that numerators are the same, if the denominator is smaller, the fraction is bigger. *A smaller denominator means the pieces of the pie are bigger.*

6. **A**

Column A	Column B
$\dfrac{1}{8} + \dfrac{5}{8}$	$\dfrac{2}{16} + \dfrac{9}{16}$
$\dfrac{1}{8} \times \dfrac{2}{2} + \dfrac{5}{8} \times \dfrac{2}{2}$	
$\dfrac{2}{16} + \dfrac{10}{16}$	

7. If you multiply the numerator and denominator of a fraction by the same number, you create an equivalent fraction!

   B

Column A	Column B
54	Total amount Ava spent in dollars if she spent $20.50 on a shirt, $30.50 on a dress, and $4 on a snack
	20 + 30 + 4 = 54
	0.50 + 0.50 = 1
	$55

8. **B**

Column A	Column B
The fraction of the pizza left if the family ate 5/6 of the pizza 1/6 which is much less than half	The fraction of cake left if the family ate 4/7 of the cake 3/7 which is almost half

9. **C**

Column A	Column B
Round to the nearest hundred: 406. 400	$1600 \div 4$ $16 \div 4 = 4$ *So...* $1600 \div 4 = 400$ 400

10. **A**

Column A	Column B
54×5 54 five times	$54 + 54 + 54 + 54$ 54 four times

11. **C**

Column A	Column B
The value of x $4x = 16$ *4x means* $4 \times x$ $4 \times 4 = 16$ $x = 4$	The value of y $12 - y = 8$ $12 - 4 = 8$ $y = 4$

12. **A**

Column A	Column B
$3 + 2 \times 5$ *Multiplication First* $3 + 10$	$(3 + 2) \times 5$ *Parenthesis First* 5×5

13. C

Column A	Column B
12 × 8	24 × 4
12 is half of 24.	4 is half of 8.
12 × 2 × 4	12 × 4 × 2

14. B

Column A	Column B
The fraction of cake remaining if Sam gave half to Kara and one forth to Maya	$\frac{1}{5} + \frac{3}{5}$
$\frac{1}{4}$ (less than half)	$\frac{4}{5}$ (more than half)

15. C

Column A	Column B
The next whole number after 112	The next odd number after 111
113	113

16. A

Column A	Column B
LCM of (5, 7)	GCF of (30, 10)
Lowest common multiple is 35	Greatest common factor is 10

When in doubt, choose the lowest common multiple.

17. **A**

	Column A	Column B
	The distance around the shape if each side is 4 inches	The distance around the shape if each side is 4 inches

Column A	Column B
4 sides that are each 4 inches	3 sides that are each 4 inches

18. **A**

Column A	Column B
$1600 - 540$	$1599 - 640$
$1600 - 540$	$1600 - 640$
Here we are subtracting 100 less than in Column B.	Here we are subtracting 100 more than in Column A.

19. **B**

Column A	Column B
$5 \times 8 \times 4 \times 0 \times 2$	3×2
Anything times 0 is 0.	6
0	

20. **B**

Column A	Column B
The value of x	The value of y
$6 + x = 22$	$y \div 2 = 9$
$22 - 6 = 16$	$9 \times 2 = 18$
$x = 16$	$y = 18$

21. **A**

Column A	Column B
The next prime number after 5 *A prime number can only be* *divided by 1 and itself.* 7	$\sqrt{36}$ 6

22. **B**

Column A	Column B
1.2×6	2.8×3
Break it up to compare. $1.2 \times 3 \times 2$	*Break it up to compare.* $1.4 \times 2 \times 3$
OR try: $12 \times 6 = 72.$	OR try: $28 \times 3 = 84.$

23. **C**

Column A	Column B
0.8×10	80×0.1
$0.1 \times 8 \times 10$ 8	$8 \times 10 \times 0.1$ 8

24. **B**

Column A	Column B
$1^{45} + 0^{32}$	$2^3 + 0^3$
1 to the power of anything is 1.	*0 to the power of anything is 0.*
$1 + 0$	$2^3 + 0$

25. **A**

Column A	Column B
The value of x	The value of y
$x - 4 = 14$	$6 \times y = 18$
Add 4 to both sides.	Divide each side by 6.
$x = 18$	$y = 3$

26. **A**

Column A	Column B
$4.526 + 3.1$	$5.2 + 2.1$
$4.5 + 3.1$	$5.2 + 2.1$
7.6	7.3

27. **B**

Column A	Column B
$345 + 431$	$305 + 481$
345 is *40 more* than 305.	481 is *50 more* than 431.

28. **B**

Column A	Column B
The number of thousands in 4304	The number of hundreds in 2921
4304	2**9**21

29. **B**

Column A	Column B
$128 + 24$	$127 + 26$
128 is *1 more* than 127.	26 is *2 more* than 24.

30. **A**

Column A	Column B
308 − 45 − 50	200
To get down to 200 you need to subtract 108. Here, you are only subtracting 45 and 50 which is 95.	

31. **A**

Column A	Column B
436 − 48	336 + 34
Estimate: 440 − 50 = 390.	Estimate: 340 + 30 = 370.

32. **C**

Column A	Column B
The next number in the series:	6 × 6
4, 12, 20, 28, ___	36
The pattern is add 8. 28 + 8 = 36	

33. **C**

Column A	Column B
1000 meters	1 kilometer
1000 meters = 1 kilometer	

34. **B**

	Column A	Column B
	Number of angles in the shape below:	Number of angles in the shape below:

	Column A	Column B
	5 angles	6 angles

35. **A**

Column A	Column B
$\dfrac{7}{6}$	$\dfrac{1}{2}+\dfrac{1}{2}+\dfrac{1}{6}-\dfrac{1}{3}$
$1+\dfrac{1}{6}$	$1+\dfrac{1}{6}-\dfrac{1}{3}$

36. **A**

Column A	Column B
2 ½ hours	130 minutes
2 hours = 120 minutes	
½ hour = 30 minutes	
120 minutes + 30 minutes	120 minutes + 10 minutes

37. **B**

Column A	Column B
54	8 tens and 2 ones
	82

38. A

Column A	Column B
The next odd number after 63	The next even number after 63
65	64

39. B

Column A	Column B
The missing number in the series 1, 3, 9, __, 81 × 3 *is the pattern.*	The missing number in the series 22, 28, __, 40 + 6 is the pattern.
27	34

40. B

Column A	Column B
0.4	$\dfrac{4}{5}$
4/10 =Under half	Over half

41. C

Column A	Column B
20	$\dfrac{1}{3}$ *of* 60
	20 + 20 + 20 = 60
	$\frac{1}{3}$ *of* 60 = 20

42. **A**

Column A	Column B
The value of h	$\dfrac{3}{2}$
$h \times 4 = 12$	
$3 \times 4 = 12$ $h = 3$	$1\dfrac{1}{2}$

43. **A**

Column A	Column B
The area of a rectangle with a length of 2 and a width of 5	The area of a rectangle with a length of 1 and a width of 6
$Area = length \times width$	$Area = length \times width$
$Area = 2 \times 5$	$Area = 1 \times 6$
10	6

44. **B**

A five pack of chocolate bars costs $2.50

Column A	Column B
The price of one chocolate bar	$0.99
$2.50 \div 5 = 0.50$	
$ 0.50	

45. **C**

Column A	Column B
40×5	50×4
$10 \times 4 \times 5$	$5 \times 10 \times 4$

If you are multiplying by the same numbers (4 and 5) but the 0's are just switched, the answer will be the same!

46. **B**

Column A	Column B
$\dfrac{4}{5} + \dfrac{1}{5} + \dfrac{3}{5}$	2
$\dfrac{8}{5}$	
$1\dfrac{3}{5}$	

47. **B**

Column A	Column B
0.4×0.2	0.4
.08	

Multiplying by a smaller decimal will make the number smaller.

48. **B**

Sarah caught fewer fish than Anya. Sarah caught more fish than Jaden.

Column A	Column B
The amount of fish Jaden caught	The amount of fish Anya caught
Less than Sarah	More than Sarah

49. **B**

Column A	Column B
The value of 3 dimes and one nickel	The value of five nickels, one dime, and one penny
3 dimes = 30 cents 1 nickel = 5 cents	5 nickels = 25 cents 1 dime = 10 cents 1 penny = 1 cent
35 cents	36 cents

50. **B**

Column A	Column B
$4 \times 4 \times 4$	4^4
	$4^4 = 4 \times 4 \times 4 \times 4$

51. **A**

Column A	Column B
10% of 200	5% of 120
This is a higher percent of a higher number.	This is a lower percent of a lower number.

52. **B**

Data set:

$4, 5, 5, 5, 8, 8, 9, 10, 10$

Column A	Column B
The mode	The median
Mode – the number that occurs the most	Median – the middle number
5	8

53. **A**

Column A	Column B
The number in the tenths place	The number in the hundredths place
2.432	2.432
2.**4**32	2.4**3**2
4	3

54. **A**

Column A	Column B
$\sqrt{49}$	$-16 \div 2$
7	-8

55. **B**

Column A	Column B
The remainder of $44 \div 10$	2^3
	$2 \times 2 \times 2$
$10 \times 4 = 40$ with 4 remaining	8

Practice Test #2

Verbal Test #2

55 Questions – 22 Minutes

---

1. dog : animal

    A) pig : hen

    B) red : white

    C) apple : fruit

    D) grape : vine

2. depression : melancholy

    A) regret : rejoice

    B) stiff : rigid

    C) temporary : permanent

    D) union : separation

3. penguin : waddle

    A) panda : bamboo

    B) peacock : feathers

    C) fox : sneaky

    D) fish : swim

4. pit : peach

    A) sheep : lamb

    B) bulb : lamp

    C) bread : mayonnaise

    D) apple : seed

5. key : lock

     A) frog : tadpole

     B) handle : door

     C) black: blue

     D) dime: ten

6. salmon : fish

     A) compass : circle

     B) lemonade : milk

     C) maple : wood

     D) egg : scrambled

7. knives : chef

     A) airplane : pilot

     B) cello : classical

     C) puzzle : pieces

     D) ball : hockey

8. hear : ears

     A) sing : stereo

     B) see : eyes

     C) nail : screwdriver

     D) car : drive

9. tulip : flower

     A) spider : grasshopper

     B) dog : puppy

     C) Daffy : duck

     D) van : car

10. tires : circles

    A) dice : spheres

    B) hamburger : triangle

    C) snake : long

    D) postcards : rectangles

11. stars : night

    A) clouds : day

    B) day : school

    C) winter : snow

    D) morning : awake

12. octopus : tentacles

    A) coffee : mug

    B) baby : rattle

    C) horse : hooves

    D) bear : brown

13. snake : reptile

    A) mammal : frog

    B) kangaroo : marsupial

    C) tiger : reptile

    D) spider : baby

14. blue : sad

    A) green : grass

    B) yellow : sun

    C) brown : mud

    D) white : surrender

15. stubborn : uncompromising

    A) guilty : patient

    B) several : most

    C) graceful : elegant

    D) exhausted : energetic

16. bold : shy

    A) fair : biased

    B) faithful : loyal

    C) courteous : polite

    D) vulnerable : confused

17. trustworthy : dependable

    A) lively : sedate

    B) outgoing : sociable

    C) joyous : miserable

    D) serious : funny

18. liter : volume

    A) Celsius : temperature

    B) fraction : decimal

    C) inch : juice

    D) moon : gravity

19. sloth : lazy

    A) cow : moo

    B) gnat : water

    C) duckling : wing

    D) bee : busy

20. calm : tense

    A) determined : committed

    B) confident : assured

    C) brave : fearless

    D) expert : novice

21. hurricane : flooding

    A) heatwave : fans

    B) drought : rain

    C) thunderstorm : lightning

    D) dirt : mudslide

22. math : algebra

    A) anger : angry

    B) disdain : smirk

    C) science : chemistry

    D) numbers : letters

23. flour : cakes

    A) eggs : omelets

    B) fork : utensil

    C) ice : water

    D) drink : glass

24. spark : fire

    A) slip : fall

    B) bad : worst

    C) fake : lie

    D) dog : puppy

25. reporter : reports

    A) nurse : sick

    B) author : writes

    C) farmer : pigs

    D) plumber : wires

26. hair : hare

    A) sit : stand

    B) tortoise : turtle

    C) where : wear

    D) bang : buck

27. bakery : bread

    A) kitchen : stove

    B) clinic : nurse

    C) pharmacy : medicine

    D) station : train

28. bad : worst

    A) warm : warmer

    B) some : few

    C) all : none

    D) sick : sickest

29. spider : legs

    A) crab : claws

    B) bird : pecks

    C) elephant : stomps

    D) dog : wags

30. chapters : book

    A) decimals : fractions

    B) sails : wind

    C) petals : flower

    D) gems : rare

31. deer : forest

    A) bee :bumbles

    B) chicken : coop

    C) shark : ocean

    D) horse : canters

32. horse : neighs

    A) dog : fetches

    B) parrot : jungle

    C) duck : quacks

    D) dolphin : dives

33. original : authentic

    A) thankful : grateful

    B) eager : patient

    C) mature : young

    D) warm : frigid

34. cow : milk

    A) windy : turbine

    B) hive : honey

    C) seeded : soil

    D) pork : cubed

35. boat : coat

      A) fear : courage

      B) ball : cot

      C) fair : lair

      D) dear : deer

36. auto : self

      A) aqua : blue

      B) cent : penny

      C) uni : one

      D) mal : malaria

37. breakfast : morning

      A) night : sky

      B) bedtime : evening

      C) day : light

      D) winter : snowy

38. fork : utensil

      A) lamp : shines

      B) mug : drink

      C) mustard : condiment

      D) hammer : nail

39. carpenter : saw

      A) butcher : shop

      B) dentist : office

      C) plumber : wire

      D) baker : mixer

40. up : above

      A) across : diagonal

      B) down : below

      C) belong : beside

      D) forward : backward

41. can : cylinder

      A) basketball : sphere

      B) nut : bolt

      C) needle : thread

      D) eraser : mistake

42. racquet : ball

      A) rod : catch

      B) pebble : round

      C) hammer : nail

      D) mop : dirty

43. mystery : genre

      A) line : straight

      B) bike : road

      C) top : blouse

      D) kiwi : fruit

44. energetic : excited

      A) sad : depressed

      B) cotton : soft

      C) dark : black

      D) syrup : maple

45. groundhog : burrow

    A) fox : den

    B) pig : cage

    C) cattle : eat

    D) whale : river

46. accept : refuse

    A) drain : flood

    B) admit : allow

    C) broad : wide

    D) concave : indent

47. carrot : root

    A) peach : seed

    B) chicken : meat

    C) lettuce : leaf

    D) sunflower : stem

48. curtail : shorten

    A) crush : elongate

    B) hesitate : pause

    C) open : close

    D) pour : satiate

49. prongs : fork

    A) monkeys : swing

    B) mother : daughter

    C) bristles : brush

    D) rainbow : red

50. prairie : grass

    A) desert : sunny

    B) glacier : cold

    C) plateau : pointed

    D) arctic : snow

51. pig : oink

    A) pelican : plunges

    B) chipmunk : chatter

    C) snake : slithers

    D) rabbit : hops

52. tri : three

    A) quad : four

    B) un : unit

    C) dis : knot

    D) re : furbish

53. swim : pool

    A) lifejacket : boat

    B) hike : trail

    C) box : storage

    D) salt : pepper

54. strawberry : milkshake

    A) garlic : spice

    B) bed : mattress

    C) oven : stove

    D) summer : hot

55. individual : group

    A) lie : fib

    B) mix : combine

    C) war : conflict

    D) praise : criticize

Verbal Test #2 - Answers

1. C	20. D	39. D
2. B	21. C	40. B
3. D	22. C	41. A
4. B	23. A	42. C
5. B	24. A	43. D
6. C	25. B	44. A
7. A	26. C	45. A
8. B	27. C	46. A
9. D	28. D	47. C
10. D	29. A	48. B
11. A	30. C	49. C
12. C	31. C	50. D
13. B	32. C	51. B
14. D	33. A	52. A
15. C	34. B	53. B
16. A	35. C	54. A
17. B	36. C	55. D
18. A	37. B	
19. D	38. C	

Verbal Test #2 - Explanations

1. Answer: C
   A dog **is a type** of animal.
   An apple **is a type** of fruit.

2. Answer: B
   Depression **is similar to** melancholy.
   Stiff **is similar to** rigid.

3. Answer: D
   A penguin **waddles.**
   A fish **swims.**

4. Answer: B
   A pit is **in the center of a** peach.
   A bulb **in the center of a** lamp.

5. Answer: B
   A key **opens a** lock.
   A handle **opens a** door.

6. Answer: C
   Salmon **is a type of** fish.
   Maple **is a type of** wood.

7. Answer: A
   A chef **uses** knives **for work.**
   A pilot **uses** an airplane **for work.**

8. Answer: B
   We hear **with** ears.
   We see **with** eyes.

9. Answer: D
   A tulip **is a type of** flower.
   A van **is a type of** car.

10. Answer: D

Tires **are in the shape of** circles.

Postcards **are in the shape of** a rectangles.

11. Answer: A

Stars **can be seen in the sky** at night.

Clouds **can be seen in the sky** during the day.

12. Answer: C

An octopus **has** tentacles.

A horse **has** hooves.

13. Answer: B

A snake **is a type** reptile.

A kangaroo **is a type** marsupial.

14. Answer: D

Blue **represents** sadness.

White **represents** surrender.

15. Answer: C

Stubborn **is the same as** uncompromising.

Graceful **is the same as** elegant.

16. Answer: A

Bold **is the opposite of** shy.

Fair **is the opposite of** biased.

17. Answer: B

Trustworthy **is similar to** dependable.

Outgoing **is similar to** sociable.

18. Answer: A

Liter **is a unit for measuring** volume.

Celsius **is a unit for measuring** temperature.

19. Answer: D

A sloth **is a seen as** lazy.

A bee **is seen as** busy.

20. Answer: D
    Calm **is the opposite of** tense.
    Expert **is the opposite of** novice.

21. Answer: C
    A hurricane **causes** flooding.
    A thunderstorm **causes** lightning.

22. Answer: C
    A type of math is algebra.
    A type of science is chemistry.

23. Answer: A
    Flour **is an ingredient in for** cakes.
    Eggs **are an ingredient in** omelets.

24. Answer: A
    A spark **leads to a** fire.
    A slip **leads to a** fall.

25. Answer: B
    A reporter **reports.**
    An author **writes.**

26. Answer: C
    Hair and hare are **homophones.**
    Where and wear are **homophones.**

27. Answer: C
    A bakery **sells** bread.
    A pharmacy **sells** medicine.

28. Answer: D
    Worst **is the superlative of** bad.
    Sickest **is the superlative of** sick.

29. Answer: A
    A spider **has** legs **for limbs.**
    A crab **has** claws **for limbs.**

30. Answer: C
   A book **has many** chapters.
   A flower **has many** petals.

31. Answer: C
   A deer **lives in the** forest.
   A shark **lives in the** ocean.

32. Answer: C
   A horse **neighs.**
   A duck **quacks.**

33. Answer: A
   Original **is the same as** authentic.
   Thankful **is the same as** grateful.

34. Answer: B
   A cow **produces** milk.
   A hive **produces** honey.

35. Answer: C
   Boat **rhymes with** coat.
   Fair **rhymes with** lair.

36. Answer: C
   Auto- **is a root word meaning** self.
   Uni **is a root word meaning** one.

37. Answer: B
   Breakfast **happens in the** morning.
   Bedtime **happens in the** evening.

38. Answer: C
   A fork **is a type of** utensil.
   Mustard **is a type of** condiment.

39. Answer: D
   A carpenter **uses a** saw.
   A baker **uses a** mixer.

40. Answer: B

   Up **is the direction of** above.
   Down **is the direction of** below.

41. Answer: A

   A can **is in the shape of a** cylinder.
   A basketball **is in the shape of a** sphere.

42. Answer: C

   A racquet **is used to hit a** ball.
   A hammer **is used to hit a** nail.

43. Answer: D

   Mystery **is a type of** genre.
   Kiwi **is a type of** fruit.

44. Answer: A

   Energetic **is similar to** excited.
   Sad **is similar to** depressed.

45. Answer: A

   A groundhog **lives in a** burrow.
   A fox **lives in a** den.

46. Answer: A

   Accept **is the opposite of** refuse.
   Drain **is the opposite of** flood.

47. Answer: C

   A carrot **is the** root **of the plant.**
   Lettuce **is the** leaf **of the plant.**

48. Answer: B

   Curtail **is similar to** shorten.
   Hesitate **is similar to** pause.

49. Answer: C

   Prongs **are a part of a** fork.
   Bristles **are a part of a** brush.

50. Answer: D

The prairie **is covered in** grass.

The arctic **is covered in** snow.

51. Answer: B

A pig makes a noise called an **oink.**

A chipmunk makes a noise called **chatter.**

52. Answer: A

Tri **is the prefix for** three.

Quad **is the prefix for** four.

53. Answer: B

A pool **is used to** swim.

A trail **is used to** hike.

54. Answer: A

Strawberry **is a type of** milkshake.

Garlic **is a type of** spice.

55. Answer: D

Individual **is the opposite of a** group.

Praise **is the opposite of** criticize.

Quantitative Reasoning Test #2

55 Questions – 22 Minutes

1.

Column A	Column B
The value of x $7x = 28$	The value of y $16 - y = 12$

A) Column A is greater.

B) Column B is greater.

C) Columns A and B are equal.

2.

Column A	Column B
$6 + 3 \times 2$	$(6 + 3) \times 2$

A) Column A is greater.

B) Column B is greater.

C) Columns A and B are equal.

3.

Column A	Column B
14×6	28×3

A) Column A is greater.

B) Column B is greater.

C) Columns A and B are equal.

4.

Column A	Column B
Fraction of stickers left if Jayla gave $\frac{2}{5}$ to Sofie and $\frac{2}{5}$ to Kim	$\frac{1}{10} + \frac{4}{10}$

A) Column A is greater.

B) Column B is greater.

C) Columns A and B are equal.

5.

Column A	Column B
Next whole number after 202	Next even number after 201

A) Column A is greater.

B) Column B is greater.

C) Columns A and B are equal.

6.

Column A	Column B
LCM of (4,7)	GCF of (24,42)

A) Column A is greater.

B) Column B is greater.

C) Columns A and B are equal.

7.

Column A	Column B
Distance around the polygon when each side is 5 cm	Distance around the polygon when each side is 5 cm

A) Column A is greater.

B) Column B is greater.

C) Columns A and B are equal.

8.

Column A	Column B
$140 - 30$	$139 - 49$

A) Column A is greater.

B) Column B is greater.

C) Columns A and B are equal.

9.

Column A	Column B
$3 \times 16 \times 32 \times 0$	6×7

A) Column A is greater.

B) Column B is greater.

C) Columns A and B are equal.

10.

Column A	Column B
The value of x $3 + x = 32$	The value of y $y \div 2 = 16$

A) Column A is greater.

B) Column B is greater.

C) Columns A and B are equal.

11.

Column A	Column B
The next prime number after 11	$\sqrt{144}$

A) Column A is greater.

B) Column B is greater.

C) Columns A and B are equal.

12.

Column A	Column B
2.2×8	3.8×2

A) Column A is greater.

B) Column B is greater.

C) Columns A and B are equal.

13.

Column A	Column B
0.4×10	40×0.1

A) Column A is greater.

B) Column B is greater.

C) Columns A and B are equal.

14.

Column A	Column B
$1^{36} \times 0^5$	$4^3 \times 0^{16}$

A) Column A is greater.

B) Column B is greater.

C) Columns A and B are equal.

15.

Column A	Column B
The value of x $x - 6 = 36$	The value of y $2 \times y = 42$

A) Column A is greater.

B) Column B is greater.

C) Columns A and B are equal.

16.

Column A	Column B
6.32 + 4.2	9.8 + 3.2

A) Column A is greater.

B) Column B is greater.

C) Columns A and B are equal.

17.

Column A	Column B
532 + 118	522 + 178

A) Column A is greater.

B) Column B is greater.

C) Columns A and B are equal.

18.

Column A	Column B
the number of thousands in 1968	the number of hundreds in 4128

A) Column A is greater.

B) Column B is greater.

C) Columns A and B are equal.

19.

Column A	Column B
$261 + 36$	$262 + 38$

A) Column A is greater.

B) Column B is greater.

C) Columns A and B are equal.

20.

Column A	Column B
$520 - 39 - 4$	452

A) Column A is greater.

B) Column B is greater.

C) Columns A and B are equal.

21.

Column A	Column B
14×80	12×60

A) Column A is greater.

B) Column B is greater.

C) Columns A and B are equal.

22.

Column A	Column B
16 + 32 + 28 + 2	19 + 36 + 48+ 7

A) Column A is greater.

B) Column B is greater.

C) Columns A and B are equal.

23.

Column A	Column B
4 feet 6 inches	54 inches

A) Column A is greater.

B) Column B is greater.

C) Columns A and B are equal.

24.

Column A	Column B
$5^2 + 1^{16}$	$5^2 + 1$

A) Column A is greater.

B) Column B is greater.

C) Columns A and B are equal.

25.

Column A	Column B
$\dfrac{12}{16}$	$\dfrac{6}{8}$

A) Column A is greater.

B) Column B is greater.

C) Columns A and B are equal.

26.

Column A	Column B
$\dfrac{2}{7} + \dfrac{5}{7}$	$\dfrac{5}{10} + \dfrac{1}{10}$

A) Column A is greater.

B) Column B is greater.

C) Columns A and B are equal.

27.

Column A	Column B
$78	Total amount that Jada spent on 3 t-shirts that were $20 each, a movie ticket for $18, and a pair of jeans for $ 38

A) Column A is greater.

B) Column B is greater.

C) Columns A and B are equal.

28.

Column A	Column B
The fraction of pie left if the friends ate $\frac{2}{8}$ of the pie	The fraction of cake left if the friends ate $\frac{1}{4}$ of the cake

A) Column A is greater.

B) Column B is greater.

C) Columns A and B are equal.

29.

Column A	Column B
554 rounded to the nearest hundred	$1800 \div 3$

A) Column A is greater.

B) Column B is greater.

C) Columns A and B are equal.

30.

Column A	Column B
38×7	$38 + 38 + 38 + 38 + 38$

A) Column A is greater.

B) Column B is greater.

Columns A and B are equal.

31.

Column A	Column B
$562 - 63$	$452 + 40$

A) Column A is greater.

B) Column B is greater.

C) Columns A and B are equal.

32.

Column A	Column B
The next number in the pattern: 7, 10, 13, 16, __	7×11

A) Column A is greater.

B) Column B is greater.

C) Columns A and B are equal.

33.

Column A	Column B
70 centimeters	7 decimeters

A) Column A is greater.

B) Column B is greater.

C) Columns A and B are equal.

34.

Column A	Column B
$\dfrac{9}{2}$	$\dfrac{1}{2} + \dfrac{1}{2} + \dfrac{1}{2} + \dfrac{1}{2} + \dfrac{1}{2}$

A) Column A is greater.

B) Column B is greater.

C) Columns A and B are equal.

35.

Column A	Column B
3 ½ hours	210 minutes

A) Column A is greater.

B) Column B is greater.

C) Columns A and B are equal.

36.

Column A	Column B
64	5 tens 14 ones

A) Column A is greater.

B) Column B is greater.

C) Columns A and B are equal.

37.

Column A	Column B
60×5	50×6

A) Column A is greater

B) Column B is greater.

C) Columns A and B are equal.

38.

Column A	Column B
$\dfrac{1}{6} + \dfrac{3}{6} + \dfrac{3}{6}$	2

A) Column A is greater.

B) Column B is greater.

C) Columns A and B are equal.

39.

Column A	Column B
2×0.8	2

A) Column A is greater.

B) Column B is greater.

C) Columns A and B are equal.

40.

Column A	Column B
Number of faces on a cube	Number of faces on a cylinder

A) Column A is greater.

B) Column B is greater.

C) Columns A and B are equal.

41.

Column A	Column B
The value of 6 dimes and 15 pennies	The value of 3 quarters

A) Column A is greater.

B) Column B is greater.

C) Columns A and B are equal.

42.

Column A	Column B
$3 \times 3 \times 3$	3^3

A) Column A is greater.

B) Column B is greater.

C) Columns A and B are equal.

43.

Column A	Column B
20% of 500	50% of 100

A) Column A is greater.

B) Column B is greater.

C) Columns A and B are equal.

44.

Data Set: 2, 2, 2, 3, 6, 7, 7

Column A	Column B
The mode of the data set	The range of the data set

A) Column A is greater.

B) Column B is greater.

C) Columns A and B are equal.

45.

Column A	Column B
The number of hundredths in 3.145	The number of thousandths in 3.145

A) Column A is greater.

B) Column B is greater.

C) Columns A and B are equal.

46.

Column A	Column B
$\sqrt{36}$	$-10 + 1$

A) Column A is greater.

B) Column B is greater.

C) Columns A and B are equal.

47.

Column A	Column B
The remainder of $48 \div 10$	$9 \div 3$

A) Column A is greater.

B) Column B is greater.

C) Columns A and B are equal.

48.

Column A	Column B
Next odd number after 71	Next even number after 71

A) Column A is greater.

B) Column B is greater.

C) Columns A and B are equal.

49.

Column A	Column B
The missing number in the pattern 4, 8, __, 16	The missing number in the pattern 48, 36, 24, __

A) Column A is greater.

B) Column B is greater.

C) Columns A and B are equal.

50.

Column A	Column B
0.7	$\dfrac{4}{10}$

A) Column A is greater.

B) Column B is greater.

C) Columns A and B are equal.

51.

Column A	Column B
2 ½ minutes	150 seconds

A) Column A is greater.

B) Column B is greater.

C) Columns A and B are equal.

52.

Column A	Column B
15	$\frac{1}{3}$ of 45

A) Column A is greater.

B) Column B is greater.

C) Columns A and B are equal.

53.

Column A	Column B
The value of y: $6 \times y = 18$	$12 \div 3$

A) Column A is greater.

B) Column B is greater.

C) Columns A and B are equal.

54.

Column A	Column B
The area of a quadrilateral with a width of 4 centimeters and a length of 5 centimeters	The area of a quadrilateral with a width of 3 centimeters and a length of 7 centimeters

A) Column A is greater.

B) Column B is greater.

C) Columns A and B are equal.

55. A 6-pack of popsicles is $6.50.

Column A	Column B
The price of one popsicle in the pack	$0.80

A) Column A is greater.

B) Column B is greater.

C) Columns A and B are equal.

Quantitative Test #2 – Answers

1.	C	20.	A	39.	B
2.	B	21.	A	40.	A
3.	C	22.	B	41.	C
4.	B	23.	C	42.	C
5.	A	24.	C	43.	A
6.	A	25.	C	44.	B
7.	A	26.	A	45.	B
8.	A	27.	B	46.	A
9.	B	28.	C	47.	A
10.	B	29.	C	48.	A
11.	A	30.	A	49.	C
12.	A	31.	A	50.	A
13.	C	32.	B	51.	C
14.	C	33.	C	52.	C
15.	A	34.	A	53.	B
16.	B	35.	C	54.	B
17.	B	36.	C	55.	A
18.	C	37.	C		
19.	B	38.	B		

Quantitative Test #2 - Explanations

1. **C**

Column A	Column B
The value of x	The value of y
$7x = 28$	$16 - y = 12$
$7 \times x = 28$	$16 - 4 = 12$
$7 \times 4 = 28$	$y = 4$
$x = 4$	

2. **B**

Column A	Column B
$6 + 3 \times 2$	$(6 + 3) \times 2$
Multiply first!	Parenthesis first!
$6 + 6$	9×2
12	18

3. **C**

Column A	Column B
14×6	28×3
$14 \times 3 \times 2$	$14 \times 2 \times 3$

4. **B**

Column A	Column B
Fraction of stickers left if Jayla gave $\frac{2}{5}$ to Sofie and $\frac{2}{5}$ to Kim	$\frac{1}{10} + \frac{4}{10}$
$\frac{4}{5}$ given away.	$\frac{5}{10}$
$\frac{1}{5}$ left	Half
Much less than half	

5. **A**

Column A	Column B
Next whole number after 202	Next even number after 201
203	202

6. **A**

Column A	Column B
LCM of (4,7)	GCF of (24,42)
28	12

When in doubt, choose lowest common multiple.

7. **A**

Column A	Column B
Distance around the polygon when each side is 5 cm	Distance around the polygon when each side is 5 cm
5 sides that are each 5 cm	4 sides that are each 5 cm

8. **A**

Column A	Column B
$140 - 30$	$139 - 49$
More than 100	Less than 100

9. **B**

Column A	Column B
$3 \times 16 \times 32 \times 0$	6×7
0	Over 0

10. **B**

Column A	Column B
The value of x $3 + x = 32$	The value of y $y \div 2 = 16$
$3 + 29 = 32$ 29	$32 \div 2 = 16$ $y = 32$

11. **A**

Column A	Column B
The next prime number after 11	$\sqrt{144}$
13	$12 \times 12 = 144$ 12

12. **A**

Column A	Column B
2.2×8	3.8×2
Estimate. 2×8 16	Estimate. 4×2 8

13. **C**

Column A	Column B
0.4×10 $0.1 \times 4 \times 10$	40×0.1 $4 \times 10 \times 0.1$

14. **C**

Column A	Column B
$1^{36} \times 0^5$	$4^3 \times 0^{16}$
Any number times $0 = 0$	Any number times $0 = 0$

15. **A**

Column A	Column B
The value of x	The value of y
$x - 6 = 36$	$2 \times y = 42$
$42 - 6 = 36$	$2 \times 21 = 42$
$x = 42$	$y = 21$

16. **B**

Column A	Column B
$6.32 + 4.2$	$9.8 + 3.2$
$6 + 4 = 10$	$10 + 3 = 13$

17. **B**

Column A	Column B
$532 + 118$	$522 + 178$
532 is 10 higher than 522.	178 is 60 higher than 118.
	Overall, this answer will be 50 higher than A.

18. **C**

Column A	Column B
the number of thousands in 1968	the number of hundreds in 4128
1968	4**1**28

19. **B**

Column A	Column B
261 + 36	260 + 38
261 is 1 higher than 260.	38 is 2 higher than 36.

20. **A**

Column A	Column B
520 − 39 − 4	452
Estimate: 520 − 40 = 480	

21. **A**

Column A	Column B
14 × 80 14 is larger than 12. 80 is larger than 60.	12 × 60

22. **B**

Column A	Column B
16 + 32 + 28 + 2	19 + 36 + 48+ 7
	Each is larger than the number in the same place in Column A.

23. **C**

Column A	Column B
4 feet 6 inches 4 x 12 + 6 48 + 6 = 54	54 inches

24. **C**

Column A	Column B
$5^2 + 1^{16}$ 1 to the power of anything is 1. $5^2 + 1$	$5^2 + 1$ $5^2 + 1$

25. **C**

Column A	Column B
$\dfrac{12}{16}$	$\dfrac{6}{8}$ $\dfrac{6 \times 2}{8 \times 2} = \dfrac{12}{16}$

When you multiply the numerator and denominator by the same number, you get an equivalent fraction!

26. **A**

Column A	Column B
$\dfrac{2}{7} + \dfrac{5}{7}$ $\dfrac{7}{7}$ 1	$\dfrac{5}{10} + \dfrac{1}{10}$ $\dfrac{6}{10}$

27. **B**

Column A	Column B
$78	Total amount that Jada spent on 3 t-shirts that were $20 each, a movie ticket for $18, and a pair of jeans for $38 $20 + 20 + 20 + 18 + 38$ $60 + 18 + 38$ $78 + 38$

28. **C**

Column A	Column B
The fraction of pie left if the friends ate $\frac{2}{8}$ of the pie	The fraction of cake left if the friends ate $\frac{1}{4}$ of the cake $\frac{1 \times 2}{4 \times 2} = \frac{2}{8}$

29. **C**

Column A	Column B
554 rounded to the nearest hundred	$1800 \div 3$
600	$18 \div 3 = 6$ $1800 \div 3 = 600$

30. **A**

Column A	Column B
38 × 7 38 + 38 + 38 + 38 + 38 +38 + 38	38 + 38 + 38 + 38 + 38

31. **A**

Column A	Column B
562 − 63	452 + 40
Estimate: About 500	Estimate: About 490

32. **B**

Column A	Column B
The next number in the pattern: 7, 10, 13, 16, __ + 3 19	7 × 11 77

33. **C**

Column A	Column B
70 centimeters	7 decimeters
10 centimeters = 1 decimeter	
7 decimeters	

34. A

Column A	Column B
$\dfrac{9}{2}$	$\dfrac{1}{2} + \dfrac{1}{2} + \dfrac{1}{2} + \dfrac{1}{2} + \dfrac{1}{2}$
	$\dfrac{5}{2}$

35. C

Column A	Column B
3 ½ hours	210 minutes
1 hour = 60 minutes 3 hours = 180 minutes ½ hour = 30 minutes 180 + 30 = 210 minutes	

36. C

Column A	Column B
64	5 tens 14 ones
	5 tens = 50 14 ones = 14
	64

37. C

Column A	Column B
60×5	50×6
$6 \times 10 \times 5$	$5 \times 10 \times 6$

38. **B**

Column A	Column B
$\dfrac{1}{6} + \dfrac{3}{6} + \dfrac{3}{6}$	2
$\dfrac{7}{6}$	
$1\dfrac{1}{6}$	

39. **B**

Column A	Column B
2×0.8	2

Multiplying by a decimal will make the number smaller.

40. **A**

Column A	Column B
Number of faces on a cube	Number of faces on a cylinder
6 faces	3 faces

41. **C**

Column A	Column B
The value of 6 dimes and 15 pennies	The value of 3 quarters
	3 quarters = 75 cents
6 dimes = 60 cents	
15 pennies = 15 cents	
$60 + 15 = 75$	

42. **C**

Column A	Column B
$3 \times 3 \times 3$	3^3 $3^3 = 3 \times 3 \times 3$

43. **A**

Column A	Column B
20% of 500	50% of 100
10% = 50 2 x 50 = 100 20% = 100	50

44. **B**

Data Set: 2, 2, 2, 3, 6, 7, 7

Column A	Column B
The mode of the data set	The range of the data set
Mode: occurs the most times	Range: highest – lowest
2	$7 - 2 = 5$

45. **B**

Column A	Column B
The number of hundredths in 3.145	The number of thousandths in 3.145
3.1**4**5 4	3.14**5** 5

46. **A**

Column A	Column B
$\sqrt{36}$	$-10 + 1$
$6 \times 6 = 36$	-9
6	

47. **A**

Column A	Column B
The remainder of $48 \div 10$	$9 \div 3$
$10 \times 4 = 40$	3
8 left over	

48. **A**

Column A	Column B
Next odd number after 71	Next even number after 71
73	72

49. **C**

Column A	Column B
The missing number in the pattern 4, 8, __, 16	The missing number in the pattern 48, 36, 24, __
Pattern: –Add 4	Pattern: Subtract 12
12	12

50. **A**

Column A	Column B
0.7	$\dfrac{4}{10}$
7/10 More than half	Less than half

51. **C**

Column A	Column B
2 ½ minutes	150 seconds

1 minute = 60 seconds
2 minutes = 120 seconds
½ minute = 30 seconds

120 + 30 = 150 seconds

52. **C**

Column A	Column B
15	$\dfrac{1}{3}$ of 45

15 + 15 + 15 = 45
So, $\dfrac{1}{3}$ of 45 = 15

53. **B**

Column A	Column B
The value of y: $6 \times y = 18$	$12 \div 3$
	4
$6 \times 3 = 18$	
$y = 3$	

54. **B**

Column A	Column B
The area of a quadrilateral with a width of 4 centimeters and a length of 5 centimeters	The area of a quadrilateral with a width of 3 centimeters and a length of 7 centimeters
$Area = length \times width$ $Area = 4 \times 5$ 20	$Area = length \times width$ $Area = 3 \times 7$ 21

55. **A**

A 6-pack of popsicles is $6.50.

Column A	Column B
The price of one popsicle in the pack	$0.80
Each popsicle is more than $1.	

Practice Test #3

Verbal Test # 3

55 Questions – 22 Minutes

1. crow : squawk

   A)   cat : whiskers

   B)   mouse : squeak

   C)   dog : bone

   D)   elephant : peanut

2. purchase : keep

   A)   grocery : banana

   B)   borrow : return

   C)   buy : money

   D)   shopping : store

3. carpenter : wood

   A)   silk : tailor

   B)   mason : stone

   C)   astronaut : mars

   D)   doctor : hospital

4. fireman : hose

   A)   builder : saw

   B)   mathematician : politician

   C)   police : uniform

   D)   mailman : walking

5. help : assist

   A)   student : class

   B)   tutor : teach

   C)   cashier : paycheck

   D)   banker : money

6. rushing : loitering

    A)   whispering : shouting

    B)   calm : quiet

    C)   girl : little

    D)   sad : frown

7. tropical : hot

    A)   green : gold

    B)   polar : cold

    C)   sun : moon

    D)   remote : television

8. red : stop

    A)   yellow : banana

    B)   pink : princess

    C)   green : go

    D)   blue : sky

9. bee : hive

    A)   mouse : cat

    B)   ant : food

    C)   bird : nest

    D)   claw : cat

10. car : engine

    A)   night : day

    B)   member : club

    C)   frame : picture

    D)   microscope : lens

11. baker : bread

    A)   teacher : books

    B)   clerk : papers

    C)   maid : laundry

    D)   jeweler : rings

12. negative : positive

    A)   dirty : clean

    B)   mad : angry

    C)   popular : friendships

    D)   interesting : hard

13. hot : warm

    A)   cold : humid

    B)   summer : winter

    C)   hilarious : funny

    D)   big : little

14. mouse : computer

    A)   rat : house

    B)   flash : camera

    C)   television : actor

    D)   cat : chase

15. fern : plant

    A)   animal : sound

    B)   bird : flying

    C)   minnow : fish

    D)   catch : throw

16. whale : ocean

    A)   sky : high

    B)   meerkat : land

    C)   slide : children

    D)   seaweed : lake

17. cub : bear

    A)   cave : wolf

    B)   truck : car

    C)   doll : girl

    D)   joey : kangaroo

18. classes : graduation

    A)   sandwich : bologna

    B)   countdown : launch

    C)   eggs : shell

    D)   breakfast : sausage

19. peak : mountain

    A)   porch : swing

    B)   roof : house

    C)   ceiling : fan

    D)   car : engine

20. subtle : blatant

    A)   tiny : small

    B)   large : huge

    C)   quiet : loud

    D)   big : gigantic

21. elephant : mammal

    A)   dog : bark

    B)   cat : meow

    C)   eagle : bird

    D)   tree : leaf

22. cow : milk

    A)   eagle : fly

    B)   mouse : run

    C)   chicken : egg

    D)   horses : gallop

23. pants : clothing

    A)   belt : builder

    B)   shoes : feet

    C)   gloves : hands

    D)   sandwich : food

24. medicine: sickness

    A) water: dehydration

    B) politeness: correction

    C) sweetheart: disloyalty

    D) intoxicating: sympathy

25. expert : knowledge

    A)   dictator : power

    B)   contestant : participates

    C)   monarch : poverty

    D)   fool : elegance

26. hour : minutes

    A)   penny : month

    B)   nickel : round

C)   dollar : spend

D)   meter : centimeters

27. cat : tail

A)   whistle : dog

B)   earth : human

C)   hunger : potato

D)   fish : fin

28. weary : sleep

A)   food : sleepy

B)   thirsty : water

C)   night : darkness

D)   bed : blanket

29. fast : rapid

A)   soft : flat

B)   slow : sluggish

C)   long : skinny

D)   damp : hot

30. glacier: ice

A)   trestle: train

B)   dune: sand

C)   forest: pathway

D)   bird: feather

31. notes : symphony

A)   words : language

B)   stories : tales

C)   graphing : answers

D)   song : musical

32. easy : hard

    A)   difficult : tough

    B)   later : now

    C)   later : after

    D)   faulty : simple

33. scientist : telescope

    A)   farmer : tractor

    B)   chisel : cut

    C)   row : plant

    D)   plough : grow

34. climb : tree

    A)   fish : swim

    B)   swim : pool

    C)   jump : big

    D)   run : jog

35. drive : car

    A)   horse : galloping

    B)   burrow : dig

    C)   pedal : bicycle

    D)   walk : run

36. come : came

    A)   ride : rode

    B)   rode : riding

    C)   ride : ridden

    D)   come : coming

37. enormous : huge

   A)   muddy : dirt

   B)   renewed : relieved

   C)   concerned : worried

   D)   mischievous : thoughtful

38. pragmatic : practical

   A)   unclear : little

   B)   simple : uneasy

   C)   puzzling : confusing

   D)   attractive : clear

39. capture : release

   A)   persuade : sway

   B)   designate : watch

   C)   interpret : dismiss

   D)   support : contradict

40. mystery : solve

   A)   horror : chilling

   B)   race : run

   C)   lost : fountain

   D)   April : showers

41. Flake: snow

   A)   storm: hail

   B)   drop: rain

   C)   field: straw

   D)   stack: hay

42. microwave : oven

    A)   chair : couch

    B)   diner : food

    C)   palm : coconut

    D)   green : lettuce

43. perimeter: square

    A)   degree: angle

    B)   height: pyramid

    C)   circumference: circle

    D)   area : rectangle

44. author : write

    A)   judge : fair

    B)   skeptic : know

    C)   surgeon : operate

    D)   driver : car

45. spite : might

    A)   great : hate

    B)   cheer : chair

    C)   trim : grime

    D)   stare : look

46. clean : stain

    A)   sew : tear

    B)   drink : eat

    C)   acquire : get

    D)   leave : take

47. brave : courage

    A)   old : youth

    B)   rich : money

    C)   afraid : experience

    D)   game : play

48. accept : except

    A)   addition : subtraction

    B)   phase : graze

    C)   incite : insight

    D)   grasp : trap

49. one : three

    A)   five : six

    B)   three : four

    C)   five : seven

    D)   eight : eleven

50. see : saw

    A)   eat : consume

    B)   hair : hare

    C)   run : ran

    D)   dear : deer

51. tennis : doubles

    A)   singing : duo

    B)   chess : match

    C)   race : solo

    D)   soccer : striker

52. consequence : result

   A)   guard : battle

   B)   prohibit : allow

   C)   examine : inspect

   D)   desire : suggest

53. ascend : descend

   A)   build : create

   B)   healthy : strong

   C)   above : over

   D)   attack : defend

54. flag : country

   A)   hope : rainbow

   B)   heart : love

   C)   green : clover

   D)   stop : walk

55. scissors : cut

   A)   belt : worn

   B)   drink : hot

   C)   tractor : carry

   D)   needle : sew

Verbal Test #3 – Answers

1. B	20. C	39. D
2. B	21. C	40. B
3. B	22. C	41. B
4. A	23. D	42. A
5. B	24. A	43. C
6. A	25. A	44. C
7. B	26. D	45. A
8. C	27. D	46. A
9. C	28. B	47. B
10. D	29. B	48. C
11. D	30. B	49. C
12. A	31. A	50. C
13. C	32. B	51. A
14. B	33. A	52. C
15. C	34. B	53. D
16. B	35. C	54. B
17. D	36. A	55. D
18. B	37. C	
19. B	38. C	

Verbal Test #3 – Explanations

1. Answer: B
   A crow **squawks.**
   A mouse **squeaks.**

2. Answer: B
   When you purchase, you keep **the item.**
   When you borrow, you **return the item.**

3. Answer: B
   A carpenter **works with** wood.
   A mason **works with** stone.

4. Answer: A
   A fireman **uses a** hose.
   A builder **uses a** saw.

5. Answer: B
   To help **means to** assist.
   To tutor **means** to teach.

6. Answer: A
   Rushing **is the opposite of** loitering.
   Whispering **is the opposite of** shouting.

7. Answer: B
   Tropical **weather is** hot.
   Polar **weather is** cold.

8. Answer: C
   Red **means** stop.
   Green **means** go.

9. Answer: C
   A bee **lives in a** hive.
   A bird **lives in a** nest.

10. Answer: D
    An engine **is a part of a** car.
    A lens **is a part of a** microscope.

11. Answer: D

A baker **makes** bread.
A jeweler **makes** rings.

12. Answer: A

Negative **is the opposite of** positive.
Dirty **is the opposite of** clean.

13. Answer: C

Hot **is a more extreme version of** warm.
Hilarious **is a more extreme version of** funny.

14. Answer: B

A mouse **is a tool for a** computer.
A flash **is a tool for a** camera.

15. Answer: C

A fern **is a type** of plant.
A minnow **is a type** of fish.

16. Answer: B

A whale **lives** in the ocean.
A meercat **lives** on the land.

17. Answer: D

A cub **is a baby** bear.
A joey **is baby** kangaroo.

18. Answer: B

Classes **are before** graduation.
A countdown **is before** a launch.

19. Answer: B

A peak **is at the top of** a mountain.
A roof **is at the top of** a house.

20. Answer: C

Subtle **is the opposite of** blatant.
Quiet **is the opposite of** loud.

21. Answer: C

An elephant **is a type of** mammal.
An eagle **is a type of** bird.

22. Answer: C

A cow **produces** milk.
A chicken **produces** eggs.

23. Answer: D

Pants **are a type of** clothing
A sandwich **is a type of** food

24. Answer: A

Medicine **is a cure for** sickness.
Water **is a cure for** dehydration.

25. Answer: A

An expert **has** knowledge.
A dictator **has** power.

26. Answer: D

An hour **can be divided into** minutes.
A meter **can be divided into** centimeters.

27. Answer: D

A cat **has a body part that is a** tail.
A fish **has a body part that is a** fin.

28. Answer: B

If you are weary, **you need** sleep.
If you are thirsty, **you need** water.

29. Answer: B

Fast **is the same as** rapid.
Slow **is the same as** sluggish

30. Answer: B

A glacier **is made of** ice.
A dune **is made of** sand.

31. Answer: A

Notes **are a part of a** symphony.
Words **are a part of a** language.

32. Answer: B
    Easy **is the opposite** of hard.
    Later **is the opposite** of now.

33. Answer: A
    A scientist **uses a** telescope.
    A farmer **uses a** tractor.

34. Answer: B
    Climb **is an action that can be done in a** tree.
    Swim **is an action that can be done in** the water.

35. Answer: C
    To drive **is to move a** car.
    To pedal **is to move a** bicycle.

36. Answer: A
    Came **is the past tense of** come.
    Rode **is the past tense of** ride.

37. Answer: C
    Enormous **is the same as** huge.
    Concerned **is the same as** worried.

38. Answer: C
    Pragmatic **is the same as** practical.
    Puzzling **is the same as** confusing.

39. Answer: D
    Capture **is the opposite of** release.
    Support **is the opposite of** contradict

40. Answer: B
    A mystery **is meant to be** solved.
    A race **is meant to be** run.

41. Answer: B
    A flake **is a piece of** snow.
    A drop **is a piece of** rain.

42. Answer: A

   A microwave **is in the same category as** an oven.
   A chair **is in the same category as** a couch.

43. Answer: C

   Perimeter **is the distance around a** square.
   Circumference **is the distance around** a circle.

44. Answer: C

   An author **writes.**
   A surgeon **operates.**

45. Answer: A

   Spite **rhymes with** might.
   Great **rhymes with** hate.

46. Answer: A

   To clean **is the way to fix** a stain.
   To sew **is the way to fix** a tear.

47. Answer: B

   Someone who is brave **has** courage.
   Someone who is rich **has** money.

48. Answer: C

   Accept and except **are homophones.**
   Incite and insight **are homophones.**

49. Answer: C

   Three **is two more than** one.
   Seven **is two more than** five.

50. Answer: C

   Ran **is the past tense of** run.
   Saw **is the past tense of** see.

51. Answer: A

   Tennis **in a group of two is called** doubles.
   Singing **in a group of two is called** a duo.

52. Answer: C

   A consequence **is the same as** a result.
   Examine **is the same as** inspect.

53. Answer: D

Ascend **is the opposite of** descend.
Attack **is the opposite of** defend.

54. Answer: B

A flag **is a symbol for a** country.
A heart **is a symbol for a** love.

55. D

Scissors **are a tool to** cut.
A needle **is a tool to** sew.

Quantitative Reasoning Test #3

55 Questions – 22 Minutes

1.

Column A	Column B
$\dfrac{13}{12}$	$\dfrac{2}{3} + \dfrac{1}{6}$

A) Column A is greater.

B) Column B is greater.

C) Columns A and B are equal.

2.

Column A	Column B
2 feet 7 inches	31 inches

A) Column A is greater.

B) Column B is greater.

C) Columns A and B are equal.

3.

Column A	Column B
$2700 \div 3$	903

A) Column A is greater.

B) Column B is greater.

C) Columns A and B are equal.

4.

Column A	Column B
$2 \times 2 \times 2$	2^2

A) Column A is greater.

B) Column B is greater.

C) Columns A and B are equal.

5.

Column A	Column B
10% of 180	20% of 100

A) Column A is greater.

B) Column B is greater.

C) Columns A and B are equal.

6.

Column A	Column B
$472 - 60$	$320 + 73$

A) Column A is greater.

B) Column B is greater.

C) Columns A and B are equal.

7. Stephanie caught fewer fish than Alice, but more fish than Jamie.

Column A	Column B
The amount of fish Jamie Caught	The amount of fish Alice caught

A) Column A is greater.

B) Column B is greater.

C) Columns A and B are equal.

8.

Column A	Column B
$3\frac{1}{3}$ hours	175 minutes

A) Column A is greater.

B) Column B is greater.

C) Columns A and B are equal.

9.

Column A	Column B
The value of x $x - 3 = 15$	The value of y $6 \times y = 60$

A) Column A is greater.

B) Column B is greater.

C) Columns A and B are equal.

10.

Column A	Column B
The area of a rectangle with a length of 3 and a width of 5	The area of a rectangle with a length of 2 and a width of 12

A) Column A is greater.

B) Column B is greater.

C) Columns A and B are equal.

11.

Column A	Column B
The value of h when $h \times 2 = 6$	$\dfrac{5}{2}$

A) Column A is greater.

B) Column B is greater.

C) Columns A and B are equal.

12.

Column A	Column B
The number in the tenths place	The number in the hundredths place
2.3	2.38

A) Column A is greater.

B) Column B is greater.

C) Columns A and B are equal.

13.

Column A	Column B
The fraction of the pizza left if the family ate 5/8 of the pizza	The fraction of cake left if the family ate 3/6 of the cake

A) Column A is greater.

B) Column B is greater.

C) Columns A and B are equal.

14.

Column A	Column B
$3840 - 630$	$3110 - 110$

A) Column A is greater.

B) Column B is greater.

C) Columns A and B are equal.

15.

Column A	Column B
12×5	15×4

A) Column A is greater.

B) Column B is greater.

C) Columns A and B are equal.

16.

Column A	Column B
The number of thousands in 4000	The number of hundreds in 8500

A) Column A is greater.

B) Column B is greater.

C) Columns A and B are equal.

17.

Column A	Column B
The missing number in the series 1, 4, 16, ___, 128	The missing number in the Series 29, 32, _, 38

A) Column A is greater.

B) Column B is greater.

C) Columns A and B are equal.

18.

Column A	Column B
The fraction of cake remaining if Hector gave half to Liam and one fourth to Zack	$\dfrac{1}{10} + \dfrac{3}{5}$

A) Column A is greater.

B) Column B is greater.

C) Columns A and B are equal.

19.

Column A	Column B
$541 - 30 - 6$	500

A) Column A is greater.

B) Column B is greater.

C) Columns A and B are equal.

20.

Column A	Column B
0.4×10	40×0.1

A) Column A is greater.

B) Column B is greater.

C) Columns A and B are equal.

21.

Column A	Column B
$\sqrt{64}$	$-30 \div 3$

A) Column A is greater.

B) Column B is greater.

C) Columns A and B are equal.

22.

Column A	Column B
$\dfrac{7}{12}$	$\dfrac{7}{11}$

A) Column A is greater.

B) Column B is greater.

C) Columns A and B are equal.

23.

Column A	Column B
The next whole number after 56	The next odd number after 55

A) Column A is greater.

B) Column B is greater.

C) Columns A and B are equal.

24.

Column A	Column B
The remainder of $38 \div 10$	3^2

A) Column A is greater.

B) Column B is greater.

C) Columns A and B are equal.

25.

Column A	Column B
$65	Total amount Sarah spent in dollars if she spent $15.50 on a shirt, $45.50 on a dress, and $2 on a snack

A) Column A is greater.

B) Column B is greater.

C) Columns A and B are equal.

26.

Column A	Column B
The value of x $8 + x = 30$	The value of y $y \div 3 = 6$

A) Column A is greater.

B) Column B is greater.

C) Columns A and B are equal.

27.

Column A	Column B
The next number in the series: 3, 12, 21, 30, ___	6×6

A) Column A is greater.

B) Column B is greater.

C) Columns A and B are equal.

28.

Column A	Column B
The next odd number after 54	The next even number after 54

A) Column A is greater.

B) Column B is greater.

C) Columns A and B are equal.

29.

Column A	Column B
$16 + 20 + 54 + 10$	$12 + 26 + 24 + 8$

A) Column A is greater.

B) Column B is greater.

C) Columns A and B are equal.

30.

Column A	Column B
The distance around the shape if each side is 6 inches	The distance around the shape if each side is 6 inches

A) Column A is greater.

B) Column B is greater.

C) Columns A and B are equal.

31.

Column A	Column B
The value of x when $24 = 8x$	The value of y when $13 - y = 8$

A) Column A is greater.

B) Column B is greater.

C) Columns A and B are equal.

32.

Column A	Column B
$\dfrac{3}{6} + \dfrac{2}{6} + \dfrac{4}{6}$	2

A) Column A is greater.

B) Column B is greater.

C) Columns A and B are equal.

33.

Column A	Column B
1500 meters	1.5 kilometers

A) Column A is greater.

B) Column B is greater.

C) Columns A and B are equal.

34.

Column A	Column B
The number of angles in the shape below:	The number of angles in the shape below:

A) Column A is greater.

B) Column B is greater.

C) Columns A and B are equal.

35.

Column A	Column B
15×0.3	15×0.01

A) Column A is greater.

B) Column B is greater.

C) Columns A and B are equal.

36.

Column A	Column B
The next prime number after 5	$\sqrt{16}$

A) Column A is greater.

B) Column B is greater.

C) Columns A and B are equal.

37.

Column A	Column B
13×20	24×10

A) Column A is greater.

B) Column B is greater.

C) Columns A and B are equal.

38.

Column A	Column B
$1^5 + 0^9$	$2^2 + 0^2$

A) Column A is greater.

B) Column B is greater.

C) Columns A and B are equal.

39.

Column A	Column B
68	5 tens and 6 ones

A) Column A is greater.

B) Column B is greater.

C) Columns A and B are equal.

40.

Column A	Column B
52×3	$52 + 52 + 52 + 52$

A) Column A is greater.

B) Column B is greater.

C) Columns A and B are equal.

41.   Data set: 4, 4, 5, 6, 8, 8, 8, 12, 14

Column A	Column B
The mode	The median

A) Column A is greater.

B) Column B is greater.

C) Columns A and B are equal.

42.

Column A	Column B
$\dfrac{2}{3} + \dfrac{4}{3}$	$\dfrac{3}{5} + \dfrac{4}{5}$

A) Column A is greater.

B) Column B is greater.

C) Columns A and B are equal.

43.

Column A	Column B
The value of 2 quarters and one dime	The value of 6 dimes and one penny

A) Column A is greater.

B) Column B is greater.

C) Columns A and B are equal.

44.   A four-pack of chocolate bars costs $3.20

Column A	Column B
The price of one chocolate bar	$0.95

A) Column A is greater.

B) Column B is greater.

C) Columns A and B are equal.

45.

Column A	Column B
$3^2 + 1^5$	$3^2 + 1^9$

A) Column A is greater.

B) Column B is greater.

C) Columns A and B are equal.

46.

Column A	Column B
LCM of (6, 8)	GCF of (35, 50)

A) Column A is greater.

B) Column B is greater.

C) Columns A and B are equal.

47.

Column A	Column B
0.2	$\dfrac{2}{5}$

A) Column A is greater.

B) Column B is greater.

C) Columns A and B are equal.

48.

Column A	Column B
$4 + 3 \times 5$	$(4 + 3) \times 5$

A) Column A is greater.

B) Column B is greater.

C) Columns A and B are equal.

49.

Column A	Column B
$6.2 + 3.3$	$5.2 + 4.34$

A) Column A is greater.

B) Column B is greater.

C) Columns A and B are equal.

50.

Column A	Column B
$230 + 40$	$130 + 130$

A) Column A is greater.

B) Column B is greater.

C) Columns A and B are equal.

51.

Column A	Column B
20×3	30×2

A) Column A is greater.

B) Column B is greater.

C) Columns A and B are equal.

52.

Column A	Column B
20	$\frac{1}{4}$ of 80

A) Column A is greater.

B) Column B is greater.

C) Columns A and B are equal.

53.

Column A	Column B
$10 \times 0 \times 5$	4×5

A) Column A is greater.

B) Column B is greater.

C) Columns A and B are equal.

54.

Column A	Column B
$340 + 560$	$130 + 760$

A) Column A is greater.

B) Column B is greater.

C) Columns A and B are equal.

55.

Column A	Column B
2.3×4.2	1.4×3.9

A) Column A is greater.

B) Column B is greater.

C) Columns A and B are equal.

Quantitative Test #3 – Answers

1. A	20. C	39. A
2. C	21. A	40. B
3. B	22. B	41. C
4. A	23. C	42. A
5. B	24. B	43. B
6. A	25. A	44. B
7. B	26. A	45. C
8. A	27. A	46. A
9. A	28. B	47. B
10. B	29. A	48. B
11. A	30. A	49. B
12. B	31. B	50. A
13. B	32. B	51. C
14. A	33. C	52. C
15. C	34. B	53. B
16. B	35. A	54. A
17. A	36. A	55. A
18. B	37. A	
19. A	38. B	

Quantitative Test #3 - Explanations

1. **A**

Column A	Column B
$\dfrac{13}{12}$	$\dfrac{2}{3} + \dfrac{1}{6}$
More than 1	Less than 1
	$\dfrac{4}{6} + \dfrac{1}{6} = \dfrac{5}{6}$

2. **C**

Column A	Column B
2 feet 7 inches	31 inches
2 feet = 24 inches	
24 + 7 = 31 inches	

3. **B**

Column A	Column B
2700 ÷ 3	903
$27 \div 3 = 9$	
$2700 \div 3 = 900$	

4. **A**

Column A	Column B
$2 \times 2 \times 2$	2^2
	2×2

5. **B**

Column A	Column B
10% of 180	20% of 100
10% = 18 (10% is the same as dividing by 10)	10% = 10 20% = 20

6. **A**

Column A	Column B
$472 - 60$	$320 + 73$
Over 400	Under 400

7. **B**

Stephanie caught fewer fish than Alice, but more fish than Jamie.

Column A	Column B
The amount of fish Jamie caught	The amount of fish Alice Caught
Less than Stephanie	More than Stephanie

8. **A**

Column A	Column B
$3\frac{1}{3}$ hours	175 minutes
1 hour = 60 minutes 3 hours = 180 minutes	

9. **A**

Column A	Column B
The value of x $x - 3 = 15$	The value of y $6 \times y = 60$
$18 - 3 = 15$ $x = 18$	$6 \times 10 = 60$ $y = 10$

10. **B**

Column A	Column B
The area of a rectangle with a length of 3 and a width of 5	The area of a rectangle with a length of 2 and a width of 12
$3 \times 5 = 15$	$2 \times 12 = 24$

11. **A**

Column A	Column B
The value of h when $h \times 2 = 6$	$\dfrac{5}{2}$
$3 \times 2 = 6$ $h = 3$	$6 \div 2 = 3$ *So, $5 \div 2$ is less than 3*

12. **B**

Column A	Column B
The number in the tenths place 2.3	The number in the hundredths place 2.38
2.**3** 3	2.3**8** 8

13. **B**

Column A	Column B
The fraction of the pizza left if the family ate 5/8 of the pizza	The fraction of cake left if the family ate 3/6 of the cake
3/8 Less than half	3/6 Half

14. **A**

Column A	Column B
$3840 - 630$ $3800 - 600 = 3200$	$3110 - 110$

15. **C**

Column A	Column B
12×5	15×4
60	60

16. **B**

Column A	Column B
The number of thousands in 4000	The number of hundreds in 8500
4000 4	8**5**00 5

17. **A**

Column A	Column B
The missing number in the series 1, 4, 16, ___, 128 Pattern: × 4 64	The missing number in the series 29, 32, __, 38 Pattern: +3 35

18. **B**

Column A	Column B
The fraction of cake remaining if Hector gave half to Liam and one fourth to Zack	$\frac{1}{10} + \frac{3}{5}$
Less than half left	More than half

19. **A**

Column A	Column B
$541 - 30 - 6$	500
$541 - 36$ Over 500	

20. **C**

Column A	Column B
0.4×10	40×0.1
$0.1 \times 4 \times 10$	$4 \times 10 \times 0.1$

21. **A**

Column A	Column B
$\sqrt{64}$	$-30 \div 3$
$8 \times 8 = 64$ 8	$30 \div 3 = 10$ $-30 \div 3 = -10$

22. **B**

Column A	Column B
$\dfrac{7}{12}$	$\dfrac{7}{11}$

Given that numerators are the same, if the denominator is smaller, the fraction is bigger. A smaller denominator means the pieces of the pie are bigger.

23. **C**

Column A	Column B
The next whole number after 56	The next odd number after 55
57	57

24. **B**

Column A	Column B
The remainder of $38 \div 10$	3^2
	3×3
$3 \times 10 = 30$ 8 remaining	9

25. **A**

Column A	Column B
$65	Total amount Sarah spent in dollars if she spent $15.50 on a shirt, $45.50 on a dress, and $2 on a snack
	$15 + 45 = 60$ $2 + 0.5 + 0.5 = 3$ 63

26. **A**

Column A	Column B
The value of x	The value of y
$8 + x = 30$	$y \div 3 = 6$
$8 + 22 = 30$	$18 \div 3 = 6$
$x = 22$	$y = 18$

27. **A**

Column A	Column B
The next number in the series:	6×6
$3, 12, 21, 30, \_\_$	36
Pattern: +9	
39	

28. **B**

Column A	Column B
The next odd number after 54	The next even number after 54
55	56

29. **A**

Column A	Column B
$16 + 20 + 54 + 10$	$12 + 26 + 24 + 8$
54 is much higher than any number in column B.	The 54 in column A outweighs the smaller differences.

30. **A**

Column A	Column B
The distance around the shape if each side is 6 inches	The distance around the shape if each side is 6 inches

| Four 6-inch sides | Three 6-inch sides |

31. **B**

Column A	Column B
The value of x when $24 = 8x$	The value of y when $13 - y = 8$
$24 = 8 \times 3$ $x = 3$	$13 - 5 = 8$ $y = 5$

32. **B**

Column A	Column B
$\dfrac{3}{6} + \dfrac{2}{6} + \dfrac{4}{6}$ $\dfrac{9}{6}$ Less than 2	2

33. **C**

Column A	Column B
1500 meters	1.5 kilometers

1000 meters = 1 kilometer
500 meters = 0.5 kilometers
1.5 kilometers

34. **B**

Column A	Column B
The number of angles in the shape below:	The number of angles in the shape below:

5 angles

6 angles

35. **A**

Column A	Column B
15×0.3	15×0.01

The smaller the decimal, the smaller the number will become when multiplied.

36. **A**

Column A	Column B
The next prime number after 5	$\sqrt{16}$
7	$4 \times 4 = 16$
	4

37. A

Column A	Column B
13×20	24×10
$13 \times 2 = 26$ $13 \times 20 = 260$	240

38. B

Column A	Column B
$1^5 + 0^9$	$2^2 + 0^2$
$1 + 0$	$4 + 0$

39. A

Column A	Column B
68	5 tens and 6 ones 56

40. B

Column A	Column B
52×3 $52 + 52 + 52$	$52 + 52 + 52 + 52$

41. C

Data set: 4, 4, 5, 6, 8, 8, 8, 12, 14

Column A	Column B
The mode	The median
8	8

42. **A**

Column A	Column B
$\dfrac{2}{3} + \dfrac{4}{3}$	$\dfrac{3}{5} + \dfrac{4}{5}$
$\dfrac{6}{3}$	$\dfrac{7}{5}$
2	Less than 2

43. **B**

Column A	Column B
The value of 2 quarters and one dime	The value of 6 dimes and one penny
2 quarters = 50 cents 1 dime = 10 cents 60 cents	6 dimes = 60 cents 1 penny = 1 cent 61 cents

44. **B**   A four-pack of chocolate bars costs $3.20

Column A	Column B
The price of one chocolate bar $3.20 for four	$0.95 About 4 dollars for four

45. **C**

Column A	Column B
$3^2 + 1^5$	$3^2 + 1^9$
$3^2 + 1$	$3^2 + 1$

46. **A**

Column A	Column B
LCM of (6, 8)	GCF of (35, 50)
Lowest Common Multiple: 24	Greatest Common Factor: 5

47. **B**

Column A	Column B
0.2	$\dfrac{2}{5}$
$\dfrac{2}{10}$	

48. **B**

Column A	Column B
$4 + 3 \times 5$	$(4 + 3) \times 5$
$4 + 15$	7×5
19	35

49. **B**

Column A	Column B
$6.2 + 3.3$	$5.2 + 4.34$
$6.2 + 3.3 = 9.5$	9.54

50. **A**

Column A	Column B
$230 + 40$	$130 + 130$
270	260

51. **C**

Column A	Column B
20×3	30×2
60	60

52. **C**

Column A	Column B
20	$\frac{1}{4}$ of 80
	$20 + 20 + 20 + 20 = 80$
	$\frac{1}{4}$ of $80 = 20$

53. **B**

Column A	Column B
$10 \times 0 \times 5$	4×5
0	

54. **A**

Column A	Column B
$340 + 560$	$130 + 760$
900	890

55. **A**

Column A	Column B
2.3×4.2	1.4×3.9
Estimate: $2 \times 4 = 8$	$1 \times 4 = 4$

SCAT Scoring

How Scoring Works

Scores

Because the SCAT is a gifted exam, students are compared to those two grade levels above their current grade. Students will receive a percentile score and a scaled score.

When you test matters

When you test makes a difference! If you are testing in the winter, the cut off score is two points lower if you test before January 1st than if you test after. If you are testing in the summer, it is best to test before June 30th. Before June 30th, you are testing for the grade you just finished. After June 30th, you are testing for the grade you are going into.

Estimating your Scores

The scoring of the SCAT is scaled and can vary based on the test you took.

Five of the questions are experimental and do not count toward the score.

Cut Off Percentages

You can use this chart to *estimate*, but results will vary based on the test.

	Verbal	Quantitative Reasoning
2nd Grade – July - Dec	58%	60%
2nd Grade – Jan - June	62%	64%
3rd Grade – July - Dec	68%	70%
3rd Grade – Jan - June	72%	74%

Visit us online!

For more test prep materials, visit us at LarchmontAcademics.com